The Art of Darkness:

Meditations on the Effect of Horror Fiction

The Art of Darkness:

Meditations on the Effect
of Horror Fiction

W.J. Renehan

2013
New Street Communications, LLC
Wickford, RI

Published 2013 by
New Street Communications, LLC
Wickford, Rhode Island
newstreetcommunications.com

This book is dedicated to my friends and family,
for seeing me through my own horrors.

Much Love.

Note on the text:

Film dates are a reflection of the author's preference,
and therefore *not* to be considered comprehensive.

Introduction:

Why We Turn to Horror

"My belief is that art should not be comforting; for comfort, we have mass entertainment and one another. Art should provoke, disturb, arouse our emotions, expand our sympathies in directions we may not anticipate and may not even wish."

- Joyce Carol Oates

"But the apparent delight with which we dwell upon objects of pure terror, where our moral feelings are not in the least concerned, and no passion seems to be excited but the depressing one of fear, is a paradox of the heart, much more difficult of solution."

- John Aikin and Anna Laetitia Barbauld

Why is it that we so often turn to works of horror fiction as a source of entertainment when they should, by all rights, turn us off completely? Why should we pay good money to be scared out of our wits? The most obvious answer to this would be the adrenaline rush we get from it, but to chalk up the attraction of horror to this alone would be to only skim the surface of the genre's dark waters. Works of horror have myriad implications when considered from psychological, sociological, and philosophical standpoints, and perform numerous functions in regard to both personal and collective experience. Allowing for the simultaneous gratification and abreaction of tabooed desire, the simultaneous fracture and reinforcement of social, sexual, and moral codes, such fiction has persisted in cultures the world over as a stabilizing force—a means of fostering both individual and collective growth while also acting to maintain the status quo. The benefits of horror are undoubtedly subtle and largely overlooked, yet their value cannot be overstated. Before we delve into the means by which horror fiction affects us, let us first develop a clearer conception of its ends.

As a state of intense physical and cognitive agitation, horror is capable of temporarily inducing what is known as regression, in which one reverts to an earlier, more primitive stage of psychological development as a means of coping with overwhelming fear/anxiety. Horror fiction provides a kind of psychic relief in this manner, in that it allows for the experience of fear without presenting any actual physical or psychological threat. Valdine Clemens notes that "Such fiction provides an antidote for the excessively cerebral consciousness, the devitalized state that Thomas Hardy called 'the ache of modernism' and to which D.H. Lawrence referred—anticipating modern media jargon—with the term 'talking heads'" (*Return of the Repressed*, 2). As an atavistic experience, horror serves to reconnect us with our primal selves, provides temporary respite from the droning conditions of modern life, and facilitates a process of self-reevaluation in regard to the conditions of our existence. The initial shock is merely the tip of the iceberg.

Images of horror fascinate due to their effect as representations of what psychoanalysts term the "uncanny"—repressed desires of the personal and collective unconscious. As Noël Carroll asserts, "the horrific images of this genre represent compromise formations. Their repulsive aspects mask and make possible various sorts of wish fulfillment, notably those of a sexual sort" (*The Philosophy of Horror*, 170). Shock and repulsion are simply the price we must pay in order to play out these repressed desires, and thus horror fiction generates a kind of cognitive dissonance, in which we find images/situations to be foreign, yet familiar; repulsive, yet attractive; disturbing, yet somehow intriguing. This paradox is essential to understanding the various benefits of the genre's effect, as it explains why we would subject ourselves to such material in the first place. Unhealthy impulses/desires are effectively discharged in a controlled manner through vicarious stimulation.

But horror fiction acts not only as a release valve for underlying psychical pressure; such works also address everyday fears common to the human condition—areas of unease such as mortality, Apollonian/Dionysian conflict, social strife, anxieties concerning sexuality and reproduction, etc. By affording us the opportunity to confront these subjects in a *controlled* manner, horror fiction acts as counter-phobia, focusing fear as a means of overcoming it. This is akin to the process of habituation, in which a person comes to respond less intensely to a stimulus in the wake of repeated exposure to it. Many variables come into play, and there is no guarantee that such exposure won't result in further sensitization—therefore some people find nothing beneficial in the effect of horror fiction. But assuming we do respond in a positive manner, it is within the power of such works to help us become better adjusted, happier individuals.

Aside from its cathartic aspects and ability to renew personal and collective perception, horror fiction also works on a more obvious, unsettling level. At the forefront of consciousness, even though we aren't likely to admit it, we know we like to participate in the weirdness—even if only in a passive sense. Stephen King acknowledges that "[Horror] offers us a chance to indulge in deviant, antisocial behavior by proxy—to commit gratuitous acts of violence, indulge our puerile dreams of power, to give in to our most craven fears" (*Danse Macabre*, 43). On a base level, the attraction of horror is not unlike that of a sexual fetish—deviously intriguing. Therefore it seems no coincidence that such fiction frequently expresses themes of sadism, masochism, unnatural and seemingly insatiable lust, physical and emotional degradation, and so on. In fact, our most firmly established horror figures and conventions are absolutely loaded with sexual energy (a topic we will expand on in chapter three). Ever found yourself rooting for a monster/violator? Sure you have. Now ask yourself why that is.

Continuing this line of thought, while horror fiction effectively lifts the constraints of social, sexual, and moral codes for our entertainment, it simultaneously reinforces the established order as well. (This should come as no surprise, as fear has been employed throughout human history as an effective means of control, both oppressive and motivational. Right wing employment of fear of the outsider or "other" is a classic example.) Appearing in cultures the world over and frequently corresponding with Jungian archetypes, horror images and narratives have roots in various mythical and spiritual belief systems. By depicting the horrific consequences of indulging in unproductive, tabooed behavior, such fiction is socially instructive; a mechanism for perpetuating the laws and values of the collective. Thus the young woman who becomes a bit too familiar with the men folk finds herself deceived by a demon in disguise. The man who attempts to play God deludes himself, his efforts resulting in abomination and ruin. Those who push too far beyond the boundary of that which is known come to pay a terrible price. James B. Twitchell notes that "These sagas, while not necessarily making the right predictions about future life, are memory banks of social and sexual possibilities both for the individual and the group. They show exactly what will melt down the nuclear family" (*Dreadful Pleasures*, 104). In that they are prescriptive as well as entertaining, works of horror present themselves as a fascinating means of maintaining societal order.

But works of horror fiction act not only as a means of coping with the anxieties of a particular culture or era; they also function as a means of responding to such anxieties. As Michael J. Collins points out, "[Horror] acts as the voice of every successive generation, and tailors its approach accordingly" (*A Dark Night's Dreaming*, 121). For example: more recent works of horror clearly reflect a heavy postmodern influence. These stories have become increasingly self-referential, emphasizing a sense of tradition in response to the ever more fragmented and compartmentalized conditions of modern life. Also, the ever more graphic depictions of violence and gore in such fiction can be seen as representative of the devalued conception of the individual in the modern world. The focus has turned more and more toward the complete and utter helplessness of the individual in the larger scheme of the universe, existing at the mercy of forces beyond control.

If anything is absolutely certain about works of horror fiction, it's that they touch us in a very personal way, and what we take away from that experience—whether positive or negative—is very much our own. (This is a very special phenomenon in a day and age when people go about their lives in a relatively numb and detached state. To feel anything, even fear, is like a breath of fresh air—invigorating, rejuvenating. Fear is a wonderful reminder that we are indeed alive.) Aside from allowing for escape from the confines of modern life, and providing an outlet of release for underlying psychical pressures, horror fiction has the power to facilitate personal and collective change in anticipation of the future. Such works have a great deal to teach us if we are willing to open ourselves to the experience, and if the price of that knowledge is a little scare, then so be it.

The Art of Darkness

Chapter One:

Momento Mori

"The boundaries which divide Life from Death are at best shadowy and vague. Who shall say where the one ends, and where the other begins?"

- Edgar Allan Poe, "The Premature Burial"

"Yesterday, upon the stair,
I met a man who wasn't there
He wasn't there again today
I wish, I wish he'd go away."

- Hughes Mearnes, "Antigonish"

Mortality is of course one of the most obvious and commonly evoked themes in horror fiction, and therefore a fine place to begin our study of its effect. Death presents itself as that which is ultimately unknowable, and the thought of what may lie across that dark chasm frightens and fascinates us in a base, primal sense. Even small reminders of our fragility as mortals, such as fictional depictions of death and dying, are laden with emotion, eliciting a sense of terrible awe in even the most jaded of individuals. Further, as Dr. Robert Kastenbaum notes in his book *The Psychology of Death,* there exists a line of scholarly thought that connects all fears to the base one of death. "According to this view, then, fear of anything is, at its root, a death-related fear. The relationship just happens to vary in its visibility and directness from fear to fear," (42). It stands to reason then that controlled encounters with death-stimuli, as a form of what psychologists refer to as "exposure therapy," might result in decreased levels of fear and anxiety towards it—and therefore foster a healthier understanding of its nature. Fictional representations of death afford us such a means of controlled approach, allowing us to meet death in our own time, on our own terms. In this chapter we will explore the various dimensions of mortality in horror fiction in order to develop a more rounded conception of its effect.

To begin, it should be noted that a great deal of our anxiety regarding death results from our inability to discuss it in a meaningful manner. Whereas past civilizations embraced death with a sense of community and purpose, the tendency of modern culture—particularly Western culture—has been to keep it out of sight and out of mind. This has resulted in an increased sense of spiritual fragmentation and isolation among individuals, further devaluing the connection between the individual and larger society. Valdine Clemens notes: "the past, present, and future, the dead and the living, are no longer felt to be vitally connected as they formerly were in less technologically advanced societies," (*Return of the Repressed,* 5). Thus horror fiction, in its ability to facilitate a process of psychological regression, helps to remedy this sense of cultural dislocation. In pulling back the death shroud, such fiction allows us to circumvent its surrounding cultural stigma, which only serves to accentuate its negative aspects. To conceptualize death as a negative is to dehumanize a natural feature of the life cycle, and to anticipate the

Flatliners, 1990

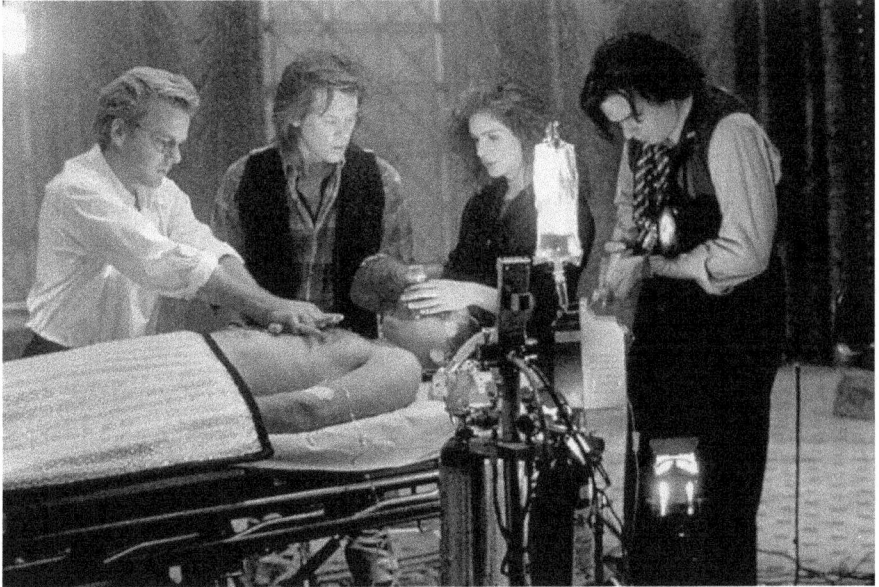

IT, 1990

Event Horizon, 1997

The Exorcist, 1973

inevitable with fear instead of acceptance is to deny ourselves the pleasure of living—of having lived at all. Take the film *Jacob's Ladder* (1990) for instance. Seemingly a nightmarish take on Ambrose Bierce's short story "An Occurrence at Owl Creek Bridge" (1890), the film's entire action centers around a man's psychic struggle against the onset of death, his mind generating an alternate reality in which he is relentlessly pursued by demons. What should rightly be a peaceful transition is turned into a nightmare.

As Elizabeth Kübler Ross points out in her classic study *On Death and Dying*, we walk around with a loose conception of death, yet "it is inconceivable for our unconscious to imagine an actual ending of our own life here on earth," (16). The inherent unwillingness of man to accept the inevitability and finality of death, and the pain resulting from such stubbornness, has of course been a central theme of the horror genre since its beginnings—the most common representations being those stories involving the loss of a loved one. Tales such as W.W. Jacobs's short story "The Monkey's Paw" (1902) and Stephen King's novel *Pet Sematary* (1983, film 1989) present death in a cold, objective manner—at best as a symptom of some universal balancing act, its meaning inaccessible to us. As Tony Magistrale notes of King's work in particular: "(he) repeatedly dramatizes, from an evolving perspective, the dilemma in which we find ourselves: we are without resources before the imminence of our own deaths and the catastrophe of the deaths of those we love," (*A Dark Night's Dreaming,* 4). As the audience, we identify with the characters' rebellion against a natural scheme that has robbed them of their loved ones, yet at the same time we are horrified by their ability to overlook abomination through the blindness of grief.

In a similar vein, horror fiction frequently depicts the disastrous consequences of man's hubris in trying to cheat death. As a variation of the overreacher plot, we are quite familiar with this type of story: the young man of science who fancies himself worthy of universal secrets, usurping the power of God/nature and ultimately bringing ruin upon himself and those whom he holds dear. Mary Shelley set the standard for such figures in the fevered and impulsive character of Victor Frankenstein, tapping fears surrounding the rapid advance of science and medicine and inspiring generations of writers up to this very day. H.P. Lovecraft's later meditation on Shelley's "pale student of unhallowed arts" resulted in his own disturbingly effective tale of deranged science, "Herbert West—Reanimator" (1922), pushing the bounds of abomination even further. More recently we have seen the concept of death explored in a more existential manner, such as in the Joel Schumacher film *Flatliners* (1990), and Dean Koontz's novel *Hideaway* (1992, film 1995).

Perhaps an even more psychologically potent dimension of death in horror fiction is the physical one, the varied depictions of bodily disintegration remaining the most natural, base manifestations of mortality. Missing limbs, rotting flesh, exposed organs—general categorical incompleteness. The projection of the body as temporary, our fragile vehicle from womb to tomb, which has pervaded the genre since its beginnings, has only grown more effective in a culture increasingly obsessed with the preservation of vitality and physical beauty. The power of these images is such that simple manipulations of the natural form, like sunken, rotting eyes, achieve horrific effect without any great song and dance. The natural image, to borrow the Imagist sentiment, would seem the most adequate symbol in regard to depictions of mortality. Further, the mere suggestion of physical decay is quite effective without any graphic detail. Like the thought of Dorian Gray's portrait, tucked away in a dark room, aging and deforming while the man himself remains youthful and unspoiled; or the idea of Norman Bates caring for his mother's shriveled corpse as if it were alive. The notion of the body as one's temple is a noble one, but of course even the most grand of temples will eventually crumble.

In terms of archetype, death comes to manifest itself in myriad forms—darkness, absences, images of decay and degradation, all fostering a sense of helplessness and bleak inevitability in the face of the void. But aside from asserting the transient nature of life and the inevitable failure of the body, horror fiction also comes to address death in a more direct manner—by animating/personifying it in various forms and allowing it to literally reach out to characters. Representations of death in cultures throughout history have assumed varied forms—animal/man, male/female, young/old, beautiful/repulsive, complex/featureless—reflecting not only the beliefs and values of a particular culture, but also the perceptions of individuals therein. Not unlike traditional representations of death, recent years have shown a trend toward more self-reflective monsters in horror fiction, frequently appearing as expressions of repressed guilt and/or ignorance of past transgressions, and possessing unnatural knowledge of their victims. Take for instance the spectral figures of Peter Straub's novel *Ghost Story* (1979), the shape-shifting creature in Stephen King's *IT* (1986, film 1990), or the malevolent force of the film *Event Horizon* (1997). The personalized nature of such aberrations comes to reaffirm the subjective nature of death, as something we must ultimately face on our own.

Of course, the implied existence of supernatural beings/forces beyond comprehension carries with it a whole host of philosophical and religious implications in regard to the nature of life and death. For example, the horror of William Peter Blatty's novel *The Exorcist* (1971, film 1973) lies not in the physical possession itself, but rather in the confirmation of evil's existence. ("Your mother's in here with us, Karras. Would you like to leave a message? I'll see that she gets it.") As Blatty himself notes of the real-life exorcism that inspired his novel, "if there were evil spirits, why not good? Why not a soul? Why not life everlasting?" Questions of heaven, hell, and limbo come into play: punishment for past transgressions, the possibility of eternal damnation. John Fearnley writes in his essay "Notes on the Psychology of Horror," "Almost every absolute suggests horror... Even the Absolute whom we have been taught to love inspires a feeling of awe which is removed from horror only by the fraction of a hair's breadth," (422). Man has forever dwelt upon the possibility of an afterlife, and the thought of death as a beginning is as equally horrifying as it is awe inspiring. One may escape the haunted house or the cursed town, but it is impossible to outrun the cold reach of death—and whatever it may bring.

The power/draw behind fictional representations of death ultimately lies in the mysterious, inaccessible nature of the thing itself. It stands among the greatest of unknowns; a dark waterfall, its bottom unseen until we edge upon its mighty crest. Stephen King himself has referred to the tale of horror as our "rehearsal for death," (*Danse Macabre*, 380), an effective means of coping with its finality. Indeed—as momento mori, horror fiction allows us to face the harsh reality of death by proxy, and therefore helps us to come to better terms with it.

The Art of Darkness

Chapter Two:

The Divided Self

"Horror is the removal of masks."

- Robert Bloch

"Ourself behind ourself, concealed—
Should startle most—
Assassin hid in our Apartment
Be Horror's least."

- Emily Dickinson, (670)

The duality of man is a perpetual wellspring of psychic tension, inescapable and undeniable, and therefore an eternal centerpiece of the horror tradition. The theme comes to manifest itself not just in character, but in setting as well—isolated, claustrophobic environs representative of the human psyche, in which confrontation with dark forces is simply inevitable. What is the haunted house after all but a symbol for the haunted mind? Valdine Clemens points out "The dark tunnels and underground passages of Gothic edifices represent descent into the unconscious, away from the socially constructed self and toward the uncivilized, the primitive" (*Return of the Repressed*, 7). Whether through natural or supernatural phenomena, naïve or unreliable narrators, settings, etc, Apollonian/Dionysian conflict inevitably rears its head in horror fiction, forging a psychically charged connection between rational and irrational drives, moral restraint and wonton malevolence, superego and id. In this chapter we will explore the nature of the divided self as represented by works of horror.

Whether we admit it or not, there exists a part of our psyche that envies the Dionysian abandon of monsters/violators. Considering neither moral boundaries nor the consequences of their actions, such figures embody our darkest impulses and desires, speaking to us in a regressive, primal manner. Tony Magistrale notes of these characters, "The civilized human gives way to the wolf, the educated man to the violent murderer, and the urbane psychiatrist to the cannibal. In each case, the monster represents some aspect of a repressed self transformed into the Other" (*A Dark Night's Dreaming*, 4). Natural representations, save perhaps for split-personality characters, express this duality as a static inner struggle with blurred dividing lines—while supernatural representations tend to deal more in absolutes. Archetypal figures such as the werewolf/transformation monster and the doppelganger/monstrous double allow for the physical manifestation of the divided self.

A key concept in regard to the analysis of the divided self in horror fiction is fission, a form of monstrous impurity in which there exists a temporal or spatial division between opposing identities/characters. As Noël Carroll notes of this, "[temporal fission] divides the fantastic being into two or more (categorically distinct) identities that alternatively possess the body in question"—like Jekyll and Hyde—whereas "[spatial

Psycho, 1960

Scanners, 1981

The Dark Half, 1993

American Psycho, 2000

fission] distributes the categorical conflict over space through the creation of doubles"(46)—like Thad Beaumont and George Stark in Stephen King's *The Dark Half* (1989, film 1993). Such manipulations are amply suited for the portrayal of oppositional energies—good/evil, sanity/madness, love/hate. Robert Louis Stevenson's employment of temporal fission in the character(s) Jekyll/Hyde is disturbingly effective in that it presents the inner struggle of the modern man turned outward—a Victorian werewolf. The attraction of the story, as James B. Twitchell rightly observes, "is not that it is a cautionary tale... but that it is a sensational playing-out of buried desire... made allegorical in the manner of pornography—it projects repressed desire not to censure it, but to experience it" (*Dreadful Pleasures*, 241). As personifications of unconscious desire, figures such as Hyde command our attention—they are the id loosed upon the world.

While supernatural/fantastic elements allow for more dramatic renderings of the divided self, natural depictions seem to hit closer to home in their subtle menace. Robert Bloch's novel *Psycho* (1959, film 1960) is a perfect example of this, utilizing the split personality concept to great effect. Stephen King notes of the work, "Psycho is effective because it brings the Werewolf myth home. It is not outside evil, predestination; the fault lies not in our stars but in ourselves. We know that Norman is only outwardly the Werewolf when he's wearing Mom's duds and speaking in Mom's voice; but we have the uneasy suspicion that inside he's the Werewolf all the time" (*Danse Macabre*, 85). Here Apollonian and Dionysian extremes are clearly articulated through the lens of a psychological disorder rather than supernatural phenomena, putting a very human face on some seemingly inhuman behavior. Here the monster is *au naturel.*

The vulnerability to madness is undoubtedly a source of psychic tension for all rational beings, and the fear of losing that essential measure of control is certainly a recurring concept in horror. Roger Corman has likened such loss of control to "the recreation of childhood fears, childhood fantasies" (*The Horror Café*, 1990), the recognition of our helplessness before the towering mysteries of existence. (Charles Manson, in one of his more lucid moments, rather eloquently compared total paranoia to total awareness.) Of course, some of the most exemplary explorations of madness in literature employ the use of unreliable first person narrators—certain works of Edgar Allan Poe, for example. "The Tell-Tale Heart" (1843), "The Black Cat" (1843), "The Cask of Amontillado" (1846)—by placing us in the narrators' confidence, by allowing personal insight into their thought processes, the author forges a psychic connection between character and reader; and the deeper that connection, the closer the relation, the more effective the tale. For we recognize the essential humanity of the violator before we fully understand his horrific exploits. Notable modern examples of the unreliable/unstable narrator in horror include the characters of Quentin P., the deranged killer of Joyce Carol Oates's novel *Zombie* (1995), and Patrick Bateman of Bret Easton Ellis's *American Psycho* (1991, film 2000). Bateman is particularly intriguing, as he comes to represent not just a single disturbed individual, but an entire schizophrenic culture, injecting references to and thoughtful meditations on 80's pop music/trends into the narrative between horrific murders and sickeningly debauched behavior. The first person narrative window into these characters' perspectives serves to humanize them in our eyes. They are not monsters by design; they are monsters by circumstance.

An extension on the Apollonian/Dionysian conflict inherent in man is of course the dual nature of his works—science and technology as mechanisms for both great good and unspeakable evil, serving to magnify both the best and worst of mankind. Mary Shelley's *Frankenstein* (1818) can be considered the true prototype of the Technohorror line, a subgenre that has grown wildly popular in recent years. As Anthony J. Fonseca and June Pulliam note, "Technohorror exists at the polar opposite of utopian science fiction... Where futurism is eternally optimistic, technohorror is pessimistic" (*Hooked on Horror,* 183). One vein of this subgenre includes those stories in which man's physical and/or mental abilities are augmented/magnified through scientific means—and inevitably come to accentuate the darker side of human nature. Notable works of this breed include Curt Siodmak's *Donovan's Brain* (1942, film 1953), John Farris's *The Fury* (1976, film 1978), Stephen King's *Firestarter* (1980, film 1984), and David Cronenberg's *Scanners* (film 1981). Perhaps even more disturbing are those works in which our scientific and technological creations, as inheritors of man's flawed and self-obsessed nature, decide to turn against their creators. Dean Koontz's novel *Demon Seed* (1997) puts a particularly frightening spin on this concept. In the story, the world's first self-aware artificial intelligence finds its way into a woman's computerized home security system, taking her hostage. The intelligence, superior to man but reflecting his imperfect nature, soon succumbs to the desires of the flesh, impregnating the woman with an artificial fetus, so that it may be born into the world of the senses—and begin a master race. In all-too-human form, the intelligence focuses solely on the justification of its ends, ignoring the horrifying means through which they are attained.

As Friedrich Nietzsche once wrote, "The further development of art is bound up with the duality of the Apollonian and the Dionysian, just as reproduction depends upon the duality of the sexes, their continuing strife and only periodically occurring reconciliation" (*The Birth of Tragedy*). The duality of man, as an inherent feature of works of horror fiction, comes to manifest itself in various forms through various means, but its ends are always of the same effect. Such works force us to turn inward, revealing aspects of our inner selves that we were not aware of, or perhaps did not wish to recognize, and in doing so invite us to embrace our frightening and conflicted nature as emotional, sentient beings.

The Art of Darkness

Chapter Three:

Festival of the Flesh

"I don't believe there is a horror myth in the West that is not entangled with the theme of procreation."

- James B. Twitchell, *Dreadful Pleasures*

"If I cannot inspire love, I will cause fear, and chiefly towards you, my arch enemy, because my creator, do I swear inextinguishable hatred. Have a care; I will work at your destruction."

- Mary Shelley, *Frankenstein*

The underlying sexual dimension of horror images/conventions, regardless of authorial intent and audience perception, lies at the heart of their psychological allure. Consider the modern horror movie audience for example—composed mainly of teenagers and young adults in the prime of their reproductive years, and predominately male. Why should that be? Looking back, ask yourself why the advent of the slasher film should coincide with the second wave of the Women's movement in the 60's and 70's. As manifestations of repressed, unconscious desire, the imagery and situations presented in works of horror are pornographic by nature; expressions of power play, sadomasochistic tendencies, and Dionysian abandon taken to extremes that would be considered unacceptable in the real world. Sexual energy possesses its own transformative power; power not wholly unlike that of fear. Indeed, the psychological connection between fear and arousal runs deep, as the control centers for sex and aggression in the brain are shown to be closely linked. The sexual undercurrent of horror, more blatant now than ever before, is by no means a new feature of the genre—yet it remains largely unnoticed by horror audiences/readers. In this chapter we will expand upon this frequently overlooked dimension of horror fiction.

But, you'll say, there seems nothing particularly sexual about the monsters/violators of horror fiction; and perhaps on the surface you're right. But if we dig a bit deeper and consider the core nature of such beings, it becomes quite clear that they are indeed highly sexual on a base level. In fact, our most prevalent and enduring horror figures owe a great deal of their vitality and longevity to their underlying sexual sway. Whether succumbing to their animal nature under a full moon, demanding a mate of a flawed and frightened creator, or killing in order to facilitate some kind of metamorphosis, such figures seethe sexual energy. Take the vampire for example: "Jung believed that the vampire image could be seen as an expression of what he termed the 'shadow,' those aspects of the self that the conscious ego was unable to recognize" (*The Vampire Book*, 550). As the embodiment of infantile, narcissistic behavior, this nocturnal stalker is undoubtedly sexual, caring only for its own gratification through the exploitation and abandon of others, while at the same time evoking concepts of oral fixation, forced penetration, fluid exchange, and disease transmission. We must also consider these monsters/violators in terms of

Alien, 1979

Hellraiser, 1987

The Silence of the Lambs, 1991

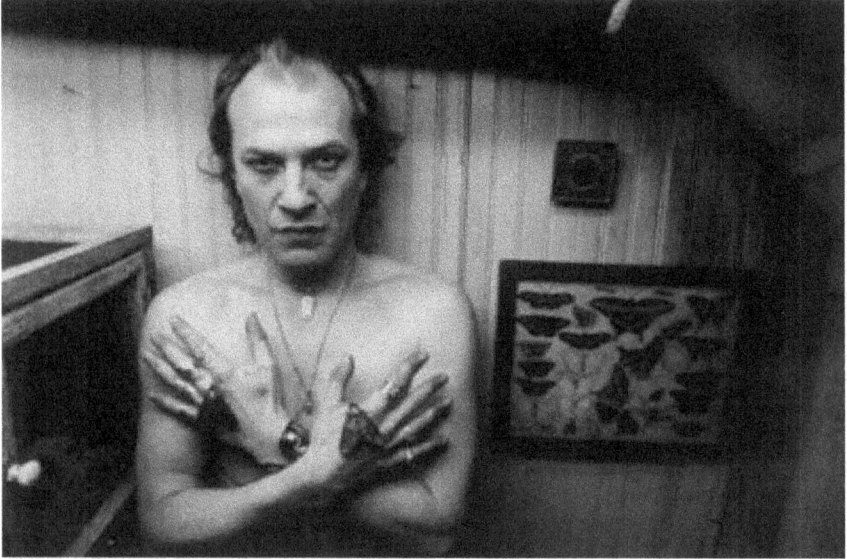

The Brood, 1979

anxieties regarding sexual potency. As manifestations of misdirected libidinal energy, such figures are impulsive and short sighted—dead set on the pursuit of their twisted ends; yet their monstrous nature renders them insatiable, forever unfulfilled. Dracula's hunger is eternal, Dr. Jekyll needs Hyde to get his rocks off, Frankenstein's monster destroys his entire family because it is denied a mate, and so on.

A more obvious sexual aspect of horror fiction would be the anatomies of monster/violators. Consider the creature from the film *Alien* (1979) with its various stages of development. From the hideous rape-like impregnation of its host, its grotesque chest-bursting birth, to its monstrous full grown form, the creature displays many vaginal and phallic attributes. As Valerie Clemens points out, "In the case of the full-fledged monster, the feature that is highlighted is the 'vagina dentata'... a copiously salivating, gaping maw that exposes not one but two and three sets of fangs" (*Return of the Repressed*, 216.) The sexual symbolism of horror figures extends beyond the physical form into modes of attack as well— such as the phallic knife thrust, strangulation, parasitic attachment, aggressive penetration, etc. The power of such imagery seems to perpetually oscillate between the implied vulnerability of the flesh and the mechanical coldness of the primal rape scene.

Aside from their underlying psychological current and physical attributes, horror figures also have sexual implications of a more practical, instructive nature. They speak to anxieties concerning social and moral codes of reproductive behavior by depicting the horror resulting from unproductive, tabooed activities. A classic example of this would be the demon lover theme. Variations of this archetypal corruptor were employed to keep young girls in sexual check long before a version was ever set to paper. There has of course been a distinct bend toward female victimization in horror fiction dating back to its beginnings, but recent years have shown an evolving reversal of this dynamic. In Michael Oliveri's novel *Deadliest of the Species* (2001), a man finds himself at the mercy of an entire town full of women. Author Thomas Harris, as Tony Magistrale points out, has effectively experimented with both male and female centers for his works. "The narrative action of *Red Dragon* [1981] is completely male generated... *The Silence of the Lambs* [1988], on the other hand, embodies an altogether different gender perspective; the women in this book are not isolated victims. In fact, they band together to fight both their isolation and victimization" (A *Dark Night's Dreaming*, 36). The playing field is being leveled, and this phenomenon can be attributed not only to women's empowerment, but also to the emergence of the LGBT community in horror. Gender categories in fiction are increasingly destabilized, and the results have been both liberating and refreshing. All is fair game.

Not only have alternative sexualities begun to find their voices in the genre, but we have also seen the emergence of unconventional sexual practices in horror, particularly those of the BDSM community—due in part to both their provocative nature and common misunderstandings concerning their employment. (*Note*: BDSM is frequently misunderstood to be a deviant culture—but that is certainly not the case. Such behavior is consensual, and therefore *not* torture. Any fictional representations to the contrary are merely artistic renderings designed to push the envelope.) Considering that evoking feelings of power and helplessness in a *controlled* manner is what horror fiction is really all about, the inclusion of/reference to such preferences/behaviors in horror seems only natural, and should not be read as a negative, but rather a positive—a testament to their psychological power. That being said, let us consider Elfride Jelinek's novel *The Piano Teacher* (1983, film 2001). Sexually charged and highly provocative, the novel depicts the development of an emotionally unstable woman's sadomasochistic relationship with one of her music students, which escalates precipitously into rape and mutilation. A far more extreme example would be Clive Barker's novella *The Hellbound Heart* (1986), which served as the basis for the film *Hellraiser* (1987). In the story, a man who has become desensitized to the pleasures of this world turns himself over to interdimensional beings said to hold the keys to unknown sensual delights. What he does not know is that their commitment to sadomasochism is so extreme in nature that they no longer differentiate between pleasure and pain. (One of the film's taglines was "There are no limits.")

We cannot conclude our analysis of sexuality in horror fiction without noting the procreative implications. From the standpoint of reproductive fears, works of horror frequently express themes of unnatural and flawed creation as the result of irresponsible or misguided behavior.

As horror scholar James B. Twitchell notes of Mary Shelley's *Frankenstein* (1818), "Young Frankenstein's progeny becomes a monster not because he violates the demands of death like the vampire, but rather because he has not been 'mothered' properly... he has been made hideous by his creator's unwillingness to nurture" (*Dreadful Pleasures*, 175). The horror resulting from Victor's shirking of his parental duties stirs reproductive anxieties that effectively bridge the gender gap, the bastard creature laying waste to everything his father/creator holds dear. Naturally stories/films of this sort play off biological fears concerning parenthood, the anxiety surrounding the fragility of the developing fetus, the numerous things that could go awry with a pregnancy. But they also represent an assault on the ideological apparatus of the family, and thus harp on the fears concerning the breakdown of societal order. Notable works within the family-horror subgenre include Ira Levin's *Rosemary's Baby* (1967, film 1968), William Peter Blatty's *The Exorcist* (1971, film 1973), John Wyndham's *The Midwich Cuckoos* (1957, film *Village of the Damned* 1960), Wes Craven's *The Hills Have Eyes* (1977), and David Cronenberg's *The Brood* (1979).

Whether blatant or subtle, the underlying sexual energy of horror monsters/conventions is undeniable. Evolving from myth and folklore, works of horror fiction persist not only as a mode of entertainment, but also as a means of reinforcing sexual codes of conduct and therefore perpetuating cultural stability in regard to reproductive behavior. But of course, as such fiction is reactive as well as prescriptive, the incorporation of alternative sexualities/orientations into the mix has served not only to enrich the horror field, but to open further social dialogue on such matters. Works of horror, despite their negative connotations, are in reality a uniting factor—melding the personal experience with the collective.

The Art of Darkness

Chapter Four:

Eat the Johnsons

"Is it better for a man to have chosen evil than to have good imposed upon him?"

- Anthony Burgess, *A Clockwork Orange*

"At most times it lies far in the back of my mind, a mere distant cloud, a memory, and a faint distrust; but there are times when the little cloud spreads until it obscures the whole sky. Then I look about me at my fellow-men; and I go in fear. I see faces, keen and bright; others dull or dangerous; others, unsteady, insincere,—none that have the calm authority of a reasonable soul. I feel as though the animal was surging up through them; that presently the degradation of the Islanders will be played over again on a larger scale."

- H.G. Wells, *The Island of Dr. Moreau*

One step beyond the horror of the self is of course the inevitable horror of the collective. As imperfect beings, our potential for good is exceeded only by our potential for evil. War, genocide, social upheaval—from the outside looking in, our species is indeed a frightening anomaly of nature. "Drug use is up, marriages down; political corruption is everywhere; bigotry's on the rise; the environment is killing us—if we don't kill it first" (*Understanding Social Problems*, 519). Evolved enough to develop language, to better ourselves through knowledge, to cure disease, to unite the world in global communication; but fearful enough of one another to hoard and hate and build unspeakable weapons to bring one another to heel. Horror fiction, by revealing the holes in our social and moral fabric, reflects the fragility of the "civilized" world, and stirs the beast beneath the business suit. The message is simple: our societal structures and the rules we wrap them in are just as fallible as we are, and the security they provide is in large part imagined. We pay little mind to the free radicals that move quietly about us; deviants, murderers, cults, psychotics. And even more frightening, the knowledge that, under the right circumstances, we ourselves may become the monster—or perhaps already have. It is no coincidence that upswings in the proliferation of horror fiction tend to coincide with periods of increased social anxiety; in fact, the two seem inextricably linked. In this chapter we will consider various themes and works in exploring the darker side of human relations, and in doing so we shall acquaint ourselves with the perilous nature of the perceived social "order."

Let us begin with a quick jaunt through one of the most frequented territories in all of literature—that of the small town. As a literary device, this societal microcosm, this bubble of humanity, serves as a natural isolation/observation tank for human relations. Such an environment is a world unto itself, but small enough to be explored and articulated intimately. When properly utilized by a writer, the small town setting can draw a reader in very effectively, creating the genuine illusion of safety—a lull before the storm. Shirley Jackson's frequently anthologized short story "The Lottery" (1948) is a prime example of the small town horror. In depicting the selection and ritual sacrifice of a woman as a village's yearly blood rite, the story explores the dangers of conformity and the duality of man. Its dreadful elegance, once past the twist ending, lies in the casual

The Wicker Man, 1973

The Stepford Wives, 1975

The Hitcher, 1986

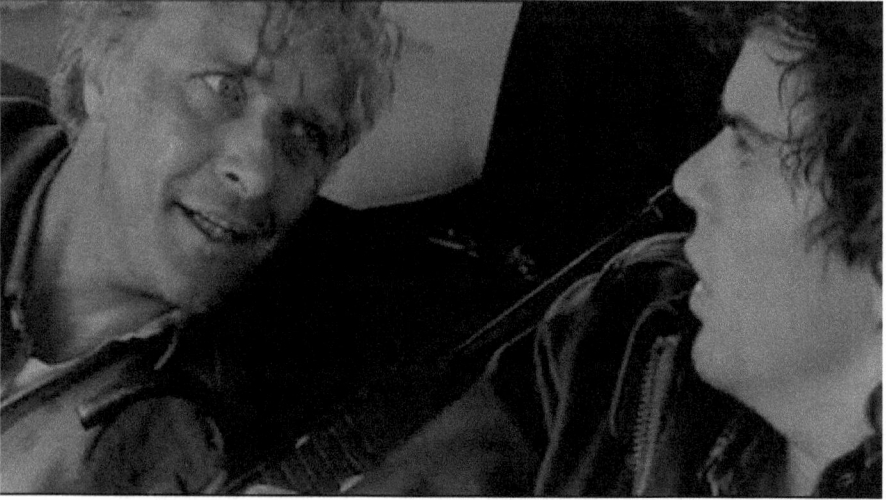

Audition, 1999

manner by which the villagers approach their barbaric task—gathering dutifully in the village square amidst an atmosphere of gossip and routine, going about a senseless act of violence in a highly sensible way. In the same vein, David Pinner's novel *Ritual* (1967), which served as the basis for the film *The Wicker Man* (1973), explores the strange practices of an isolated community, but mainly from the perspective of an outsider. Drawn into a web of sexual intrigue and debauched hallucinatory encounters with eccentric villagers, a Scotland Yard detective soon finds himself questioning not only his faith, but his sanity as well. Both "The Lottery" and *Ritual* house dueling effects; they emphasize the suffering of the outsider, and at the same time invite us to join in on their destruction—reminding us of the relative youth and fragility of our social organization.

The small town/isolated community setting is often employed in conjunction with variations on what Noël Carroll refers to as the "complex discovery plot," in which characters must go through a series of realizations in confirming the existence of a threat. Through this process, the author is afforded the time and space to generate an atmosphere of growing tension and unease, and also to develop any pertinent themes. Take for instance Ira Levin's novel *The Stepford Wives* (1972, film 1975). The story, in leading up to Joanna Eberhart's discovery that the neighboring housewives of Stepford have been replaced by subservient lookalike robots, taps into themes of gender, female oppression, misogyny, and the insidious nature of patriarchal society. The small town/isolated community setting also comes to magnify social concerns by putting a sympathetic human face on them. For example: Jay Anson's *The Amityville Horror* (1977, film 1979) carries a rather strong socio-economic subtext, the humble Lutz family purchasing a cheap house with a sordid history in order to bring their American dream to fruition. Stephen King notes "The movie might as well have been subtitled *The Horror of the Shrinking Bank Account… The Amityville Horror*, beneath its ghost-story exterior, is really a financial demolition derby" (*Danse Macabre*, 144).

Regardless of scale, tales of collective horror can ultimately be reduced to a few key points: disintegration of social, sexual, and moral codes, and the breakdown of the family unit. But aside from these, works of horror emphasize the danger of the individual in the increasingly self-absorbed and detached flurry of today's fast-moving society, where truly unstable characters can move about relatively unnoticed. As Tony Magistrale notes, it is ironic that "the criminal sociopath establishes the closest affinity yet between audience and monster... he externalizes our awareness of imminent societal collapse, the demise of values, the illusoriness of security, and our rage at being unable to change any of this," (*A Dark Night's Dreaming*, 7). There are many notable examples of this persona in literature and film, a particularly chilling one being Rutger Hauer's haunting portrayal of serial killer John Ryder (*The Hitcher*, film 1986). Criminally insane, yet highly intelligent and manipulative, Ryder operates outside the laws of men as if he is privy to some universal secret that frees him, his cool composure lending him a false air of trustworthiness. Like *The Hitcher*, Ryu Murakami's novel *Audition* (1997, film 1999) artfully explores the horror of the unassuming stranger, while also revitalizing the ultimate wolf in sheep's clothing—the femme fatale. By arranging a mock film audition as a means of meeting intelligent and talented young women, a widower unwittingly sets his sights on a genuinely twisted individual. Blinded by affection, too late this fellow comes face to face with his lover's true nature—that of a maniacal sadist obsessed with torture and amputation. By begging the question of whether or not we can ever truly know another person, tales such as these touch a highly sensitive nerve in the human psyche.

On a larger scale, works depicting apocalyptic/dystopian futures, alternative societies, war, genocide, or just general chaos, assert the uncertainty of man's future as a result of his flawed and violent nature. Stephen King's novel *The Stand* (1978, mini-series 1994), for instance, presents the fragmentation of humanity into opposing camps in the aftermath of a man made plague. Thus the fundamental duality of the collective is made physically manifest, the innocents being drawn to Boulder, Colorado, and the sinners gathering in Las Vegas. A relatively new variation on the dystopian theme plays off the potent anxieties aroused by the threat of environmental collapse due to industrialization, pollution, and general disregard for nature. One example is Hugh B. Cave's novel *The Dawning* (2000). In the story, a band of refugees fleeing a rapidly declining society awash with drugs and violent crime seek a new life in the untouched wilds of Northern Canada. To their horror, these people find nature itself in a state of rebellion against man's existence as a result of environmental abuse. The destructive nature of mankind is effectively summed up through nature's rejection of her most troubled child.

In this chapter we have considered various social dimensions of horror fiction, but it should be noted that these are neither comprehensive nor intended to establish any sort of definitive category. A social interpretation can be made of just about any work one wishes to analyze. Ultimately it comes back to the old *U* word—*unknown*. The only thing more inaccessible and horrifying than the mystery of the self is the mystery of another, and a crowd can be a lonely place indeed.

The Art of Darkness

Chapter Five:

Monster in the Mirror

"For although nepenthe has calmed me, I know always that I am an outsider; a stranger in this century and among those who are still men. This I have known ever since I stretched out my fingers to the abomination within that great gilded frame; stretched out my fingers and touched *a cold and unyielding surface of polished glass.*"

- H.P. Lovecraft, "The Outsider"

"Monsters are real, and ghosts are real too.
They live inside us, and sometimes, they win."

- Stephen King

Having roots in cultural myth and folklore long predating the written word, the concept of monstrosity undoubtedly covers a large swath of the horror tradition. Forever opposed to that which is considered natural and understood, the definition of monstrosity has of course evolved along with human experience over time. Deformities once considered to be monstrous are now recognized as genetic defects and physical handicaps; behavior that was once equated with possession by demonic forces is now recognized as mental illness; and the same imaginative drives that once led us to witch burnings and freak shows now lead us to the bookshelf or the darkened movie theater. But what lies behind the psychic draw of the monster? Why should the shambling, nearly laughable zombie command such a large following at the present? How have figures like the vampire and the werewolf retained their vitality in the face of pop culture's rapidly shrinking attention span? To establish a stronger conception of this phenomenon this chapter will effectively deconstruct the physical and psychological attributes of horror monsters in order to cut to the heart of their effect. We'll then examine said effect through the scope of both personal and collective experience.

So what is it exactly that makes a monster? Frequently corresponding with Jungian archetypes, horror monsters have firm instinctual groundings in the collective unconscious, while also clearly expressing the repressed desires of both the individual and the group. "Freud believes there are repressions of primary narcissim that have to be re-directed by increasing social demands if we are to become acculturated. In other words, desires—sexual desires—are safely abreacted in horror so that other growth can occur," (*Dreadful Pleasures*, 77). As manifestations of repressed, anti-social/tabooed desires, horror monsters intrigue us in their ability to generate cognitive dissonance, in which we find them simultaneously foreign and familiar, repulsive and attractive, horrifying and fascinating. Tony Magistrale notes, "As an audience, we greet the horror monster with a mixture of repulsion and secret identification. While part of us is appalled by its excesses and outrages, another part gleefully identifies with its rebellion against social, sexual, and moral codes," (*A Dark Night's Dreaming*, 4). Thus, as we noted in the introduction, horror fiction allows for both the gratification and abreaction of tabooed

The Raft (Creepshow 2), 1987

The Blob, 1988

The Colour Out of Space, 1927

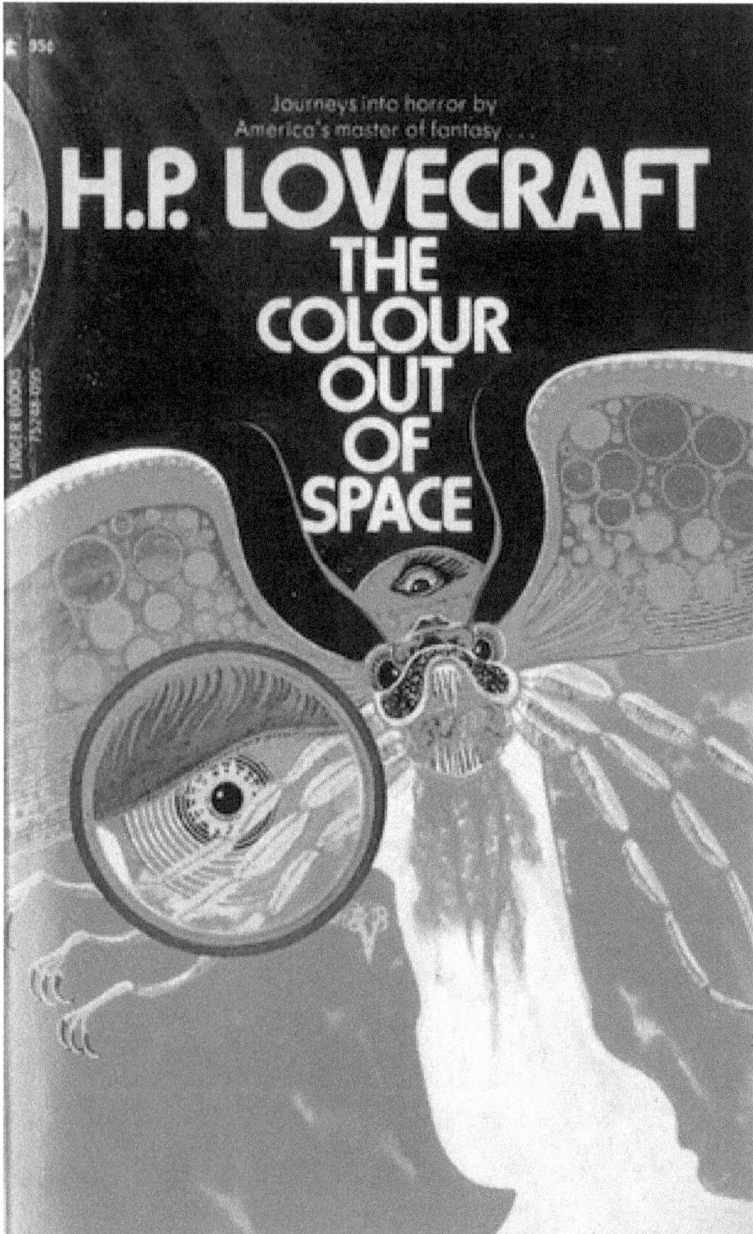

behavior/desire, the simultaneous fracture and reinforcement of the social, sexual and moral codes.

First and foremost, the monster fails to adhere to the established order of the society it invades, whether by nature or inclination. This intrusion not only disturbs said order, but also threatens to undermine it. Therefore the confrontation and destruction of the monster becomes essential to securing the balance of the perceived natural order. This is a symbolic destruction, reaffirming the established order by illustrating the horrific results of engaging in antisocial/tabooed behavior. As long as Jaws is exploded, Dracula staked, and the Overlook Hotel is burned down, we don't feel so bad about having gotten some kicks from them along the way. All is right in the world once again. There are many horror narratives that fail to offer such closure, but it would seem that the most effective ones do indeed present at least some form of resolution or respite in the clash against dark forces—for as the audience we are, at heart, essentially optimistic; longing for catharsis, reconciliation, a measure of peace. And perhaps peace is most palpable when in contrast with chaos.

Secondly, the monster's threat is typically implied through horrific impurity—deviation from/violation of our conceptual understanding of the natural. Expanding on theory expounded by Mary Douglas in her book *Purity and Danger* (1966), Noël Carroll has established what stands (in this author's opinion) as the most coherent and comprehensive breakdown of monstrous impurity. These categorical manipulations include horrific metonymy, incompleteness, massification, magnification, fusion, and formlessness. While we cannot go into all these in detail, let us expand briefly on horrific formlessness for example. Monsters that are amorphous, lacking definite shape/features are disturbing to us in a very primal sense. We are not fond of things we can't get a clear read on, and there is something very potent about the primitive fear aroused by such creatures. Stephen King's short story "The Raft" (1985, film *Creepshow 2* 1987) plays off this kind of fear to great effect by pitting a group of swimmers in an isolated lake against an amorphous, oily blob with a taste for flesh. King is obviously well aware of the primordial terror evoked by such a creature as he plays up its ability to hypnotize and draw in its prey with swirling colors along its surface. Ancient instinctual fear is triggered, and the effect is truly chilling. Another notable example of horrific formlessness would be H.P. Lovecraft's short story "The Colour Out of Space" (1927), in which a vaporous alien entity blights a farmer's land, infusing itself with vegetation, livestock and the farmer's family itself.

Thirdly, the monster presents a direct physical and/or psychological threat to both the individual and the group. Some figures offer violent bodily degradation, while others imply a subtly invasive menace, a loss of control/loss of personal or collective identity. As Stephen King rightly asserts, "it is not the physical or mental aberration in itself which horrifies us, but rather the lack of order which these aberrations seem to imply" (*Danse Macabre*, 50). Alien organisms that multiply and spread with total disregard for all other life forms, people with physical/psychic abilities that border on uncontrollable, spectral figures whose designs are unknowable, yet malicious, beings that simply fail to correspond with our established conception of nature. Consider *The Blob* for example—while the 1958 film version is your standard cheese-ball rock n' roll pep rally, the darker, more visceral 1988 remake revitalizes the concept, which is fairly sound as far as horror stories go. A seemingly mindless, gelatinous organism threatens to consume/absorb every living thing on earth—it's a truly terrifying idea. The most frightening monster is not one that is unlikely to reason, but one that simply can't reason.

Ultimately, monstrosity stands as that which does not adhere to our perception of what is right and understood in the world. Regardless of natural or supernatural properties, the monster exists as a reflection of man's relationship with his conditions of existence, an extension of his haunted and confused nature. Despite our experience and our rational, scientific minds, we remain frightened animals in the face of a universe we do not and perhaps may never understand—and the appearance of that which fails to correspond with our understanding of nature will always frighten as well as fascinate. Monstrosity, on its base level, is the antithesis of understanding.

Chapter Six:

Cthulhu and Friends

"[Horror fiction] shows us that the control we believe we have is purely illusory, and that every moment we teeter on chaos and oblivion."

- Clive Barker

"There is nothing in the dark that isn't there when the lights are on."

- Rod Serling

Since we began our study with a consideration of death, one of the great unknowns of human experience, it seems only fitting that we end by directing our attention back to the existential mystery of the universe in general. As the physician and educator Lewis Thomas once noted: "The greatest of all the accomplishments of twentieth century science has been the discovery of human ignorance." It would seem the more our sciences reveal about our place in the cosmos, the more complex the riddle of our predicament becomes. For in regard to the seemingly limitless spaces and strange phenomena of the heavens, our earthly laws and theories of universal processes fall immensely short of comprehensive understanding. The presence of supernatural elements in horror fiction, through their ability to evoke cosmic fear/awe, play upon an inherent, instinctual feature of the human psyche—our intuition that there is a great deal we do not understand, that we are perhaps incapable of understanding. From tales of unspeakable cyclopean evil to demonic possessions and ghostly happenings, that which fails to adhere to what Noël Carroll calls our "conceptual scheme of nature" presents not only a physical threat, but a cognitive one as well. In this final chapter we shall explore elements of supernatural/cosmic horror in regard to their overall effect.

As H.P. Lovecraft wrote in 1927, "All my tales are based on the fundamental premise that common human laws and interests and emotion have no validity or significance in the vast cosmos at large," (letter to Farnsworth Wright). Lovecraft, though unappreciated in his time, is now hailed as the father of modern supernatural fiction, his Cthulhu mythos achieving a standard that remains unsurpassed to this very day. Through masterful employment of variations on the complex discovery plot and a typical emphasis on atmosphere over character, Lovecraft's tales effectively depict the helpless, estranged nature of man in the universe. Humanity is frequently presented as a sort of universal runoff, a byproduct of an ancient, more advanced race that was old when the world was young. Nowhere is this more apparent than in Lovecraft's indisputable masterpiece *At the Mountains of Madness* (1936). Terry Heller notes of the work, "The general picture is of a universe of walls or frontiers. Behind each wall is an unknown world that is vitally involved in the existence and meaning of the known world, yet that may have no particular concern for the known world," (*The Delights of Terror*, 50). It is this pronounced sense

In the Mouth of Madness, 1995

'Salem's Lot, 1979

Alien, 1979

Invasion of the Body Snatchers, 1978

of universal indifference towards man that pervades tales of cosmic horror—the thought that we exist beneath the heels of cyclopean forces with little or no regard for our well being. It is no wonder that Lovecraft's narrators so often succumb to depression and madness.

A modern example of the Lovecraftian brand of cosmic horror in film would be John Carpenter's "Apocalypse" trilogy, starting with *The Thing* (1982), *Prince of Darkness* (1987), and culminating with *In the Mouth of Madness* (1995). Each work presents us with a nameless, creeping horror in the style of Lovecraft, utilizing isolated settings and unreliable characters, and threatening not only individual but collective identity. *The Thing* (1982), a rather faithful adaptation of John W. Campbell's novella *Who Goes There?* (1938), is undoubtedly the most commercially successful of the trilogy, but it is the final film *In the Mouth of Madness* (1995) that is the most successful in generating the effect of cosmic fear. We the audience are embedded with a calculating, stubborn character who is obsessed with getting to the rational heart of increasingly irrational events, the terror taking the form of a steadily increasing sense of helplessness, the intuition that confrontation with dread forces is inevitable, our struggles futile, the barriers of reality folding all around us. While the first two films attack individual and collective identity, the third simply overshadows these concerns by questioning the nature of reality.

The beauty of tales of supernatural/cosmic horror lies in their ability to provoke a strong psychological response in remarkably subtle ways. The monster need not be dragged out into light dripping with blood. In fact, what usually frightens most is not what is shown, but rather what is implied. Take *Dracula* (1897) for example—Stoker does not try to force horror on us by exploiting the vampire's fantastical/grotesque qualities. He simply hints at them from the rational perspectives of multiple characters, emphasizing the reality of the vampire's unnatural menace through the story's epistolary form. It is worth noting that the Count remains largely unseen for a fair portion of the novel, moving about his dread business behind the scenes, and allowing the reader's imagination to run wild between the shifting points of view. Written in homage to Stoker's tale, Stephen King's *'Salem's Lot* (1975, film 1979) not only builds off Stoker's framework, keeping the Master vampire in shadow for a large part of the story, but also widens the scope of the horror in terribly subtle ways. For example, before the vampire may enter the town his servant must make a sacrifice in the name of a darker, higher power in order to facilitate the passage. And later, gazing upon the house that looms above the vampire infested town, a character wonders: "Did they wander pallid through its nighted halls and hold revels, twisted services to the Maker of their Maker?" (*'Salem's Lot*, 437). The presence of evil is effectively magnified through such means. *The Maker of their Maker*—the words are cold and jarring even when taken out of context. Just what else is out there? How deep does the rabbit hole go?

Of course, supernatural/cosmic fear need not be aroused solely by fantastical beings/phenomena. After all, what is the supernatural but that which exists outside our narrow conception of the "natural." In fact, some of the most effective tales of this nature are those in which science and the unknown converge. As Valdine Clemens notes of a continuing shift in the presentation of the supernatural in Gothic fiction, "ghostly apparitions of the dead have given way to eruptions of subhuman and prehuman life forms… the organic has become a primary symbol of transpersonal reality, manifested as daemonic energy," (*Return of the Repressed,* 216). Ridley Scott's film *Alien* (1979) successfully evokes a sense of supernatural/cosmic dread while remaining within the technical realm of the possible. Stephen King himself refers to *Alien* as a supernatural tale, despite its grounding in science fiction. "I think of it as Lovecraft in outer space, mankind finally going to the Elder Gods rather than they coming to us," (*Danse Macabre*, 179). A more classic example of this brand of biological cosmic horror would be Jack Finney's novel *The Body Snatchers* (1955, film *Invasion of the Body Snatchers 1956,* 1978). Once we get around the implied subtext of Cold War hysteria, which Finney himself flatly denies, we have a straight tale of otherworldly menace, the literal takeover of a California town by body replicating aliens. Once again, the overall effect is one of complete and utter helplessness in the face of unfolding horrors.

Through means both broad and nuanced, stories of supernatural/cosmic horror ultimately, and perhaps rightly, reduce the status of mankind in the greater scheme of the universe, and force us to reevaluate our relation to it. They stand amongst the purest and most evocative works of horror fiction in generating an effect that other tales struggle to achieve. As John Fearnley notes: "Horror arising from the unnatural is as tremendous as that which comes from the supernatural, but its manifestations are less vivid, and more nearly akin to those of disgust and loathing," ("Notes on the Psychology of Horror," 426). Tales of supernatural and cosmic horror reaffirm previously shed primitive beliefs about the world and our place within it, and thus foster individual and collective growth in light of the unknown.

Bibliography:

Carroll, Noël. *The Philosophy of Horror: or Paradoxes of the Heart.*
New York: Routledge, 1990.

Clemens, Valdine. *The Return of the Repressed: Gothic Horror from The
Castle of Otranto to Alien.* New York: State University of New
York Press, 1999.

Fearnley, John. "Notes on the Psychology of Horror." The Sewanee
Review 3 (1895): 421-430.

Fonseca, Anthony J., and June Michele Pullium. *Hooked on Horror: A
Guide to Reading Interests in Horror Fiction.* Connecticut:
Teacher Ideas Press, 2003.

Heller, Terry. *The Delights of Terror: An Aesthetics of the Tale of Terror.*
Chicago: University of Illinois Press, 1987.

Kastenbaum, Dr. Robert. *The Psychology of Death.* New York: Springer
Publishing Company, Inc., 1972.

King, Stephen. *Danse Macabre.* New York: Everest House, 1981.

Kübler-Ross, Elisabeth. *On Death and Dying.* New York: Scribner, 1997.

Magistrale, Tony, and Michael A. Morrison. *A Dark Night's Dreaming:
Contemporary American Horror Fiction.* South Carolina:
University of South Carolina Press, 1996.

Melton, J. Gordon. *The Vampire Book: The Encyclopedia of the Undead.*
Detroit: Visible Ink Press, 1999.

Mooney, Linda A., and David Knox and Caroline Schacht. *Understanding
Social Problems.* California: Wadsworth, 2005.

Twitchell, James B. *Dreadful Pleasures: An Anatomy of Modern Horror.*
New York: Oxford University Press, 1985.

About the Author

W.J. Renehan is Editorial Director at Dark Hall Press, a publisher of first-quality Horror and Sci-Fi. He is an alumnus of Dean College, SUNY New Paltz and the University of Rhode Island.

New Street Communications, LLC

New Street Communications, LLC, publishes and distributes superior works of nonfiction (and, through our Dark Hall Press imprint, select fiction in the Horror genre). We are a *digital-native* imprint. As such, we primarily make our titles available as eBooks, though often in paper editions as well. On the nonfiction side of things, we cover the intersection of digital technology and society; transformative business communication and innovation (particularly the conceptualizing of elegant new tools, markets, products and paradigms); socially-relevant children's literature; and literary criticism. New Street's nonfiction books are authored by distinguished scholars, journalists, entrepreneurs, developers and thought leaders.

www.newstreetcommunications.com

www.ingramcontent.com/pod-product-compliance
Lightning Source LLC
Chambersburg PA
CBHW060610030426
42337CB00018B/3021